In the Margins

A Conversation in Poetry

In the Margins

A Conversation in Poetry

Christine Higgins
Ann LoLordo
Madeleine Mysko
Kathleen O'Toole

Dearest Ria —
With gratitude
for your
endearing
friendship,
support &
love —

Ann

Published by Cherry Grove Collections
P.O. Box 541106
Cincinnati, OH 45254-1106

ISBN: 9781625492203

Poetry Editor: Kevin Walzer
Business Editor: Lori Jareo

Visit us on the web at www.cherry-grove.com

Cover Design: Suzanne Shelden, Shelden Studios
Cover Photo: Ed Medley
Author Photo: Kevin Higgins

In the Margins: A Conversation in Poetry

Some years ago, when a young filmmaker made a documentary about our poetry group—four women midway in a decades-long journey together—we came up with a name: *In the Margins*.

In the margin of professional lives and friendships, *in the margin* of births and deaths and raising children, *in the margin* of war and resistance to war. We don't mean to suggest that the writing of poetry is peripheral to us, but rather that it is integral to those narratives.

The conversation that brought us together more than 20 years ago continues. Through it we have found the encouragement to keep writing our poems and to nurture the creative selves at the *center* of our lives — "an otherwise perfect wife" writing to resolve the dualities of her life, an unruly woman of faith coming to terms with brokenness in relationships, a working mother exploring the beauty of domesticity and the truths of the marginalized, an organizer probing the rifts within and between the human and natural worlds.

Over the years we have discovered that, though our voices remain distinct, we do share many things: our roots in the Baltimore and East Coast region, a heritage of idealism that is both generational and spiritual, and a healthy dose of both reverence and rebellion. We see, too, that our poems born of these convergences—and out of the critique of and care for each other's work—have become *shared* creations. *In the Margins* celebrates our resilience, our longevity, and the craft that holds us together.

Acknowledgments

We acknowledge and thank the journals in which some of these poems first appeared:

America: "The Naming"

Broadkill Review: "Their voices"

Ellipsis . . . Literature and Art: "On Lexington Street" and "December 26: Snowbirds Crossing Over"

Hellas: "Thursday"

Naugatuck River Review: "The Art of Gaman: The Atlanta Holocaust Museum"

Poetry East: "Empty Pockets," "Handkerchief," "Plenty," "Woman Wiping the Face of Jesus"

Rockhurst Review: "My Fortune"

Smartish Pace: "American Cortege"

The Sow's Ear Poetry Review, Fall 2015: "Community of Poets" feature included versions of the poems "In the Ofuro," "Late Season," and "Music Lesson."

"Grief" (originally entitled "Sick") was published as a composition for soprano, flute, clarinet, violin and viola by Kirk-Evan Billet (1998).

"The House, The Night of Lilacs" is included in Kathleen O'Toole's collection, *Meanwhile* (David Robert Books, 2011).

"Perpetua" and "The Naming" are included in *What Would You Die For? Perpetua's Passion* (Apprentice House, 2005).

"View Interrupted" is included in the anthology, *American Writers Respond* (Etruscan Press, 2002).

∞

We would also like to acknowledge the larger circle of women who were at one time a part of our writing circle, and with whom we continue the conversation: Joyce Stevens Brown, Bonnie Goldberg, Kim Roberts, and Natasha Sajé.

Table of Contents

testing the truth of it

what hope, what shelter

hard to believe

I

memory's the vessel

In the Ofuro

She leads me into the tiled room.
Seated on a stool, she opens the spigot
and fills a small bucket.
Dipping a cloth, she soaps her body
and gestures me to do the same.
I nearly fall off the stool;
it is so small and low.
I lather underarms, breasts,
belly, between the legs.
I avert my eyes and concentrate
on folds of flesh.

She stands, moves towards me
and begins to wash my back,
scrubbing shoulders,
passing the warm cloth
down my spine, over the hips
to the coccyx. Then a flood
spills down my back
from her bucket. She offers
me the cloth and returns to
her stool. I wash her skin,
the nape of her neck, the delicate
black hair circling like a thumbprint.

The bath is gray and solitary
this morning and the window sweats.
We are two hothouse flowers,
yellow day lily and calla
blooming in the heat.
Clean now, she motions me
to the big tiled tub. We soak,
steam circling our heads.
Side by side, we barely touch.

AL

Thursday

I have to kneel to wash my mother's feet.
Newly fragile from the surgery,
she trembles in the shower, holds on tight
to the towel bar. She's balanced slippery
as infants I have lathered in this tub.
I send a silent prayer up through the steam:
"Don't let me let her fall." I hardly scrub,
but ceremoniously overcome
the awkwardness, and move the sopping cloth
down my mother's legs, across her toes.
She thinks that she's a bother, but the truth
is I am struck with piety and lose
myself in washing her, like one ordained
to take another's precious feet in hand.

MM

Music Lesson: The Year Before She Died

I convinced her to take music lessons
from a young woman at Peabody,
who laughed delightedly
the first time she heard my daughter
sing the scales, exclaiming, *I've never*
heard anyone sing so effortlessly.

Every Wednesday afternoon,
I'd drive my daughter downtown
while she did her homework or put
make-up on in the front seat next to me.
Then we'd climb the marble staircase
and enter a darkened room
with wooden slats on the windows
and scattered wooden desks.

Danya was teaching her a song
from The Music Man, and when
I would hear the romance of it,
sweet dreams be yours, dear
if dreams there be
sweet dreams to carry you
home to me
it would bring forth tears
that would not fall or splash,
but lolled on the rim
like a note stretched out in time.

CH

Their voices

The heat — the close of another August day.
I rummage drawers of half-sleep for the voices
of my three aunts, lest time erase
the special timbre of their speech: the way

Ann's laughter endures, despite the din
of a decade's chatter, erupts in raspy
bursts — gin fizz from a barkeep's
wand. Her Lucky Strike aloft. Then

Flo died. Yet I still hear that twang
in her vowels, the wah-wah of a trumpet
solo at the Sons of Italy dance. Last, let
Ginny's cigarillo tones request a tango.

My memory's the vessel — an old jar, lid
punched with holes, to let the fireflies live.

KO

II

she comes knocking

Handkerchief

At the funeral of a colleague's wife,
I'm surprised to find it folded neatly
in the side pocket of my bag—tissue-thin cotton,
machine-scalloped edge, printed with flowers
that could be jonquils if they weren't so
impossibly blue-green, no doubt manufactured
in the fifties, but pressed upon me not long ago
by my mother, who found it too pretty
to leave behind in the consignment shop,
who must have carried it home, washed it,
laid it to dry against the side of the tub,
and ironed it into this soft and perfect square
smelling mildly of soap, which I hold
against my cheeks now, blotting the tears.

MM

Desire

My mother calls again today, a softness
in her voice, a caress in her hello
I've been waiting a lifetime to hear.
Her mind is emptying itself
like a pocketbook.

No more petty grievances:
dirty gloves on Sunday,
wrinkled shirts, unpleated skirts,
my strand of hair
that always fell without a bobby pin.
No more ritual of criticism.

From two hundred miles away
she asks have I eaten my dinner,
and how is my husband, Kevin.
I picture his name written
next to mine in the address book.
No pencil note to tell her,
before this, she never cared.

I have built up a fortress
against the injustices
and finally
she comes knocking.

CH

Late Season

She seems eager for me to prune
the buddleia, still sporting a few
grape brushes, and butterflies.

But let your father show you how...
her voice trails off. This last Sunday
of summer, the shadows lengthen

into the cooling air. Since August
the list of tasks has multiplied:
deadhead the hydrangea, cut back

the leggy rhododendron, snip
the last flowers. Prepare for spring.
As if she weren't about to lose

her love of six decades. The headstrong
boy who showed up at the stage door
to punch out her leading man

for an unscripted kiss in the senior
play; the one posing in the muscle beach
photos, composer of musical parodies,

husband into whose arms she'd swoon
in the kitchen when we kids were not
looking. Now making room

for his hospital bed in the den,
she clings to old play programs,
poems, tokens of all she feels

falling out of reach. These days
she's rehearsing new roles: nurse,
attendant. In her dreams she is

furious as the squirrels
hiding what they must preserve
before the coming frost.

KO

Lambert's Instant Guide to Birds

She sees them most mornings, alight
on the weeping cherry,
cardinal and nuthatch,
catbird and indigo bunting.
Birds of town, regular visitors
to yards and parks —
suburbanites just like her.
She spies them from the kitchen window,
and unlike the old days, she has time
to notice them now. Goldfinch or warbler
and the wren, not Carolina or common house,
but Bewick's with the white eye stripe
and a powerful, clear song
that would make even the most attentive
wife turn off the vacuum cleaner.
She's been studying them, quietly,
in between spoons of oatmeal,
following their hops, one branch to the next,
jotting down the colors and markings.
A backyard birder at 83,
she now explains her day
according to Mr. Audubon.
If this was her yard, birds would fill
the chestnut tree they had planted in '73
after Agnes uprooted the magnolia.
She would see the winter moon most nights it was full
and swoon to lemon blossoms in summer.
If this was her yard, she would know
when to water the roses and clean the barbecue.
If this was her yard, she would know
where she lives.

AL

III

pure wound of the body

Woman Wiping the Face of Jesus

Take heart daughter; your faith has made you well
Matthew 9:22

Veronica.
Notice her name is like an anagram:
Vera, Icon. Latin, Greek. True image.
They say she was invented, woven of
the stuff of relics—Jesus on a veil.

But maybe she's the woman in the gospels—
the woman with "the flow of blood," the one
untouchable. Twelve years . . . Consider how
she waited in the crowd for him to pass,

and how she let her fingers barely graze
his sleeve—the fringe, the weave's unraveling.
Consider how he turned to look at her,
and how the womb obeyed. Imagine joy,

and how she must have counted days until
the eighth, when she could buy her turtledoves
and run to have the priest declare her clean.
Veronica. Who else, there on the road

to Golgotha, elbowing through the crowd
to hold her veil against his suffering?
She takes the prize: the face of God
in human blood, impressed there, in her hands.

MM

The Naming

In a dream Perpetua beheld a bronze ladder
with swords and spears entwined around the sides,
ready to snare her if she dared not to look up.
It was the dream of a martyr, ecstatic to be dying
for her beliefs, a woman, barely a woman,
who challenged her father with the word, *Christian*.

On Halloween, when I was eight, and we were
charged by the nuns to dress as our patron saint,
my mother informed me I was named after Christ.
How that disappointed me. I wanted to dress
as St. Elizabeth in a blue veil with a bread basket of roses,
or St. Cecilia with eyeballs served up on a silver platter.

How to be like Christ?
A woman who is my patient says: My son is dead,
but before he died, I got to bathe him
head to toe, even his privates, and we weren't ashamed.
If I were climbing a ladder to heaven,
entwined in those rungs would be
all manner of things I attend to
instead of keeping an eye on my ascent:
my daughter's eyelet dress, my silk scarves, my TV set.

Disciples of Buddha say if you do not meditate
in the morning, you have wasted your morning.
St. Ignatius asks: Do you prefer life over death?

At times, I still dislike my name—*Christine*,
as if I am to be held more accountable than others.
Remember Peter who denied three times?
I'm not brave like Perpetua. I don't want
the whole damn empire to know
I am anointed, marked with the sign of faith.

CH

27

At Mount Edith Cavell Lake

My body lays itself down
on the edge of the lake.
Fresh tracks nearby.
Big-horned sheep or bear.
The bugle of an elk.
Here my body lays itself down,
impatient with life's slow pace.
Our lies swirl in the air,
repeated with each denial,
and my body lays down
as the lake beckons.
Glacial blue and steaming
it seems to call:
Forgive yourself,
the self you have become,
the ache in your side,
the self no one knows,
the stone in your mouth.
Only then will he return
to enter the pure wound of my body.

AL

The House, The Night of Lilacs

Once upstairs, I easily shed the borrowed skirt and
      tortoise-shell barrettes, like small sins
rehearsed from a catechism verse.   I could barely touch
    his skin there.
            Afterwards
     he wanted to know why I had not — protected —
did I presume — and what was braver   — then ?

Early birdsong   stealing from that novitiate
      the first Sunday of May   as Nixon sweated
toward resignation   I yielded   proudly
    rode my gentle friend,   almost maternally
as the great Cathedral bell tongued twelve.   It roused us
    rocked us   entwined with the shaking weight
of a freight train just beyond our reach

                  where this train
now passes.   The House is gone.   Removed, my secret
    monument   the pleasure each time I commuted past
as if spring rain   would forever fill the railway ditch.
                   Today
   a flat, untended lot   leaves me to invent
a stone   a leaf   as marker.   Would he
    even recall   Who   did (not) touch him
then?   Did we (either of us) leave
   a tender mark   that still aches —   a sigh
yet in the dust there   to remember ?

KO

IV

for the missing

Requiem at Compline

for K.S. 1952-2000

When I heard that you had died, I found
a deserted beach to make my peace with you.
We skirted sandpiper tracks, full moon
illuminating the tide pools around
our long running tango. The wash of waves
dissolved the last echoes of your confession,
cleared the musty relics of each transgression
I harbored, softened the hair shirt you'd woven
of small kindnesses over the years. Now
I imagine you above our bickering
voices, redeemed at last from doctors
and dialysis, free to ramble, to dowse
in a philosophers' realm, spirits flickering
in amity, without this need for words.

KO

Report from Miss Johnson, Feng Shui Consultant

Plant a garden in the missing area,
south corner of the house, the children's space.
He transplants hostas, green and white nosegays,
delicate lavender flowers on a tall, slender stem.
They will seed, the gardener says, they will multiply.

Move the couch, keep the life force flowing.
In the creative cycle, burning wood feeds fire.
She stacks oak, hickory, chestnut in a pot
beside the fireplace. Wood feeds fire;
from fire, ash, from ash, a bird rises.

Hang a white picture frame on the west wall.
Wedding picture? Traveling landscape?
Photo of an unknown couple dancing in Venice?
In China, a widow wears white, for the missing.
The wind from the west soothes like a lullaby.

Paint the bedroom; yellow frequently used
to good effect for a couple trying to have a child.
Vases of daffodils, day lilies, Alstroemeria
overtake the dresser, windowsill, nightstand.
She arrives with her arms full.

Bed is in the command position.
No adjustments necessary.
She dreams of a safari, seven days
in a Land Rover, across India,
searching for a white tiger.

House nicely protected by woods,
overlooks a large, flowing river.
He fixes a broken lock, opens
the front door, and swears he feels
the dragon's breath blowing.

Nothing happens without
consequences to something else.

AL

Grief

after "A Visual AIDS Diary" by Devorah Kleinbeast

They named it for the aftermath: *gravis* —
that heaviness. But looking back, wouldn't
you agree: The moment you would name —
the moment you first realized the loss —

was geological (the way the heart
shifted, fractured at the fault), and astral
(faith and hope and love exploding weightless,
spectacularly in, and *of,* the air)?

Splinters of song, showers of fragrant light.
Too bad you haven't got a photograph
to mount and frame in gold. But still, sometimes
against a perfect dark, haven't you seen
it floating by? The birth of Grief: *that star.*

MM

Gaman: The Atlanta Holocaust Museum

... enduring the seemingly unbearable with dignity and patience...

They could only bring what they could carry.
One hundred ten thousand Japanese
forced to "re-locate" to remote Topaz, Utah,
a spot where the sand swirled in the summer
and in the winter snow drifted through the gaps
of the whitewashed tarpaper shacks.

The women fashioned pipe cleaner flowers
which they preserved under industrial-sized mayonnaise jars;
the men painted landscapes with black ink
or created tea pots from slate;
mothers used the empty flour sacks
to make military sashes for their sons.
The red string, used for knot-gathering, dotted
the material like tiny drops of blood.

I saw such beautiful things made from their grief,
relieving my own:
a peach pit carved and polished into a ring,
painted birds in miniature
with snips of screen for their tiny feet.

CH

V

testing the truth of it

View Interrupted

from the land
there is light, more of it
though gray and ashen, plumes
filling the cathedral of the air
now a canyon, negative exposure
twin shadows replaced by light
no fixed address, this way and that
easy to lose your bearings, at canal
and sixth, a view clear south to the river

from the sea
boarding the ferry, Wall Street
bound, suits at the rail, gulls circling
in the haze, their cries overtake
the roar of engines, a droning engine
on approach not a word, to a man
not a word, uninterrupted view
interrupted, in the glare
of the sun, the Empire State
Building is what you see

from the air
a smoldering heap, the color
of ash, timbers of steel, debris
piled high, remains of the day
everlasting, the eye catches on a crane
draped in red, a tall building red
roofed, to the east, green leafy tree tops
at the edge, a marble blue river
and the long, white wake of a ferry

AL

Empty Pockets

I think of you without a cent,
without a cigarette, trouble
with your liver and your spleen,
in this heat, without
a drop of sweat left to give.

I think of you when
I slice open the cantaloupe,
and when I run my fingers
through my daughter's clean hair.
When soapy water slides across my skin
and when I slip into freshly laundered socks,
I think of you. I dive into a pool,
my arms stretched out to swim

and I think of your need,
cheeks hollowed with hunger,
head falling forward in sleep,
leathery skin, swollen ankles,
empty pockets, shoes unlaced.

In better times, you could have been
a walking Calvin Klein ad. But today,
from behind your hospital wheelchair,
I see what you see every day —
people brushing past you, faces turned away.
They can't know that after
I bummed you a cigarette, you struggled
to your feet and balanced on one good leg,
that you smiled and said, *Come on. Get in.*
It's your turn.

CH

Marching to Zion

In memoriam, Rev. Vernon Dobson, 1923-2013

At your funeral, no one's thundering
at the injustice of our loss, no one to sling

a brass-plated epithet, like you, from that pulpit –
hewn in the movement's resilience. Your wit,

now silenced. My fondest memories kept
as photos in sepia: you seated behind your desk,

head down as if brooding, before a scathing insight
carved six pounds of hubris from some politician's hide.

Or your voice, booming through the congregation's
hymnody at a public assembly, marching us to Zion

or imparting your *Blessed Assurance* with the heat
of a branding iron: *this is our story,* lest we forget.

You knew we'd be testing the truth of it before
long – too much at stake on the streets of Baltimore.

KO

American Cortege

after Cortege et Litanie, Marcel Dupré

Stand now at the curb of time, hand against
the heart: The great cortege
is passing through this hour of pause.

Crane the imagination: impossible to see
the head of the line, the first to roll
heavily past his mother's weeping eyes.

This one now: When and where was he lost,
this farm boy from Vermont?
No time to wonder—the tolling bell, the drums,

the bugle—and now he moves beyond
our view, all his sweet particulars draped
in the colors of the universal:

red for sacrifice,
white for innocence—and for absence,
blue for those dispassionate skies above the battleground.

As for the litany: impossible to name them all.
Grip the heart then for the crescendo, the weight,
the unbearable rolling on, and through.

MM

VI

what hope, what shelter

Roses, Roses, Roses

Bright red, the gift of a valentine.
Crimson red, a dozen to say
"I'm sorry, it won't happen again."
Peach roses in the front garden,
pricking the one who
dares to steal them.

Innocents dropping soft pink
petals to announce the bride.
Tea roses in the wedding bouquet.
Confetti roses, white roses
surrounded by baby's breath.

Rose petals opening,
opening, blooming like
the vagina at birth.

Dark roses, almost black,
for a dead girl's birthday.
Yellow roses blanketing the casket.
Bud roses in the shape of a rosary.

We let go of one thing
in order to see
what else there can be,
what hope, what shelter.
The priest wears a chasuble
embroidered with vines and
roses, roses, roses.

CH

Perpetua

The ladder held
spears and hooks and knives,
but I was not deterred,
not by the serpent's tooth or its venom,
for I knew beyond lay my welcome.

A garden with passion fruit
and pomegranates, prickly pears
and plums, the dark red center
of my heart. My father had hoped I would renounce
the man and be freed from the prison
at Carthage, to leave the arena unscathed,
for the sake of my son. This is the beginning
of my flowering, in all manner of speaking,
to rise up and embrace language, which will free
me from earth's fever and its dark red scent.
Even now, as they oil my body, I am anxious
to be done with the body,
for though it is comely, it is no longer mine
to give.

AL

Corinthian Baptist, First Sunday

If I silence them, even the stones will shout out.

Luke 19:39

That palpable hope – a hawk ready
to ride a wind current out over the edge –
lifts the familiar hymns a decibel
higher than the lyrics and organ notes

combined. *Something I never thought
I'd live to see,* the pastor quips, lacing
the air with expectation. Yet he stops;
and the faithful wait for anyone to name

what everyone's on the verge of – yet
all refrain, fearing it will shatter, or
ignite, as a match would in the kitchen
of a house full of dreams. Still, all

the jumpin' chords of gospel bounce
into the autumn morning, as if it *needs*
brightening, scoring the long slow burn
of pent up desire, pitch rising in each vamp

between verses – until the nodding heads,
hats, eyes seem to signify: this time *even
the stones will shout out –* if need be
in three-part harmony, to pave the way.

KO

On Lexington Street

Chafed with your own little worries on a bitter
morning in January, you shoulder out
through the doors of the crowded market, only to
collide with cutting wind, light reflected off
the filthy snow, and a sound fierce after your heart
like something animal, big and starved:
chimes, the carillon at the St. Jude's Shrine,
announcing *Great is Thy Faithfulness*.

Faithfulness . . . faithfulness, joy with teeth in it—
The hymn carries you along the street,
banging you against the drunk on the corner
and the sad-eyed child with a child on her hip,
scraping you hard against the angry amputee
in his beat-up wheelchair, then flinging you free.
Morning by morning new mercies I see—Hope
like a brush burn you could have done without.
You pull yourself brave in the face of it,
brave in the glorious, stinging cold.

MM

VII

hard to believe

My Fortune

If I could have read
a fortune, when I was alone
in my airless New York apartment,
crying over another lost love,
it would have been: *One day,*
you will drive your teenage
daughter and her friend
through a countryside of corn
and horses and handmade fences
to a church camp for city kids
where they are volunteering, and
you will sing Beatles songs
together and plan a picnic dinner.
I would have found it
hard to believe
that my life would begin,
once I'd left what I thought
was the center of the universe.

CH

Plenty

All those present ate their fill. The fragments remaining, when
gathered up, filled twelve baskets. Matthew 14:20

An autumn morning at the farmer's market
just up the road. The sunny roundness of pumpkins
echoes bright orbs of tomatoes among the last truckload
of green-husked sweet corn; eight varieties of apples
cascade from bushel baskets. Sliced samples: stayman,
winesap, empire and jana gold, line up beside
the jugs of fresh pressed cider and cozy rows
of acorn and butternut, zucchini's green fullness.

Far —but not so far — from the dusty roadsides
of Nyeri, where we passed farmers
with their plantain and pineapple stacked
on bright blankets, from the muddy market days
of Enugu, where among the traffic and shanties,
vendors hawked bananas piled high in palm baskets,
offered towering bowls of ground cassava
on makeshift tables.

And that farmer we met
in Machakos with three crates of tomatoes balanced
on his rickety bicycle, elated because the new water pan
irrigates his fields, so he can feed his family and then cart
the surplus to market each week, though it takes him
three hours down storm-rutted roads.

The hope
of abundance: plenty of time to ponder seeds and fruit,
water and tools. And to be — like the apostles — amazed
at just how many those five loaves and two fishes feed,
to take measure of the miracle, and all the fragments.

KO

51

December 26: Snow Birds Crossing Over

O the miles of orange groves dropping
less-than-perfect fruit, the ratty palms
festooned for Christmas in the rusting trailer parks,
the wistful little amusements, rusting too.
75 degrees and rising. We have arrived.

But O the wide and coldly flawless sky,
that detached blue, beneath which all the warmth
seems cowered, pressed against the ground.
Whatever lies beyond those spotless clouds
isn't glancing down, couldn't care less.

Along Route 27, a billboard shouts that Jesus
has gone to make a place for us in heaven.
O better to think of him right here
in Florida, pulling up a lawn chair beside
his aging Airstream. Loving it. Loving us.

MM

Wanda's Grove

Seek refuge in the grove of black walnuts,
the trees planted at her instructions.
Saplings shy and willowy
as she was in daddy's arms.
Go there at dusk, when twilight fades
and the dark night envelopes you
like the folds of her winter coat.

Do you remember that December,
winter of '69? You ran from the house,
crying, the dog dead in the street.
She pulled on that coat and took out
after you, found you sitting
in snow beside the walnut trees.

You ride the back roads in the truck,
hoping she has gone for one of her walkabouts.
You drive and drive, and with each far mile,
realize that you will have to climb
the hill behind the farm,
walk past forsythia, rhododendron
to find her beneath black walnuts,
calling you home.

AL

The Poets

Christine Higgins is a MacDowell Colony fellow and the recipient of Individual Artist grants from the State of Maryland in both poetry and nonfiction. Her work has appeared in numerous literary journals, including *Pequod, Little Patuxent Review, Lullwater Review,* and *PMS (poem/memoir/story)*. Her chapbook, *Threshold,* was published in 2013 by Finishing Line Press. Her most recent book, *Plum Point Folio,* is a collection of her poems and her husband's photographs. She is currently at work on a memoir about grief.

Ann LoLordo is a former Opinion Page editor and Middle East correspondent for *The Baltimore Sun* who has reported from Afghanistan, Iraq, Iran, Lebanon, Egypt, Jordan, Sudan, China, Japan, and Tanzania. Presently she is a writer-editor for an international non-profit health organization. She is a graduate of Georgetown University and the Johns Hopkins Writing Seminars whose poetry has appeared in journals that include *The Greensboro Review, The MacGuffin,* and *Puerto del Sol.* A native of New York, she lives in Annapolis with her husband and son.

Madeleine Mysko is a registered nurse and writer whose poems, stories, and essays have appeared in journals that include *Smartish Pace, The Hudson Review, Poetry East, Bellevue Literary Review,* and *Sojourners.* She is the author of two novels, *Bringing Vincent Home* (2007) and *Stone Harbor Bound* (2015). She holds advanced degrees from The George Washington University and Johns Hopkins University, and has taught creative writing in the Baltimore-Washington area for years. She serves as contributing editor at *American Journal of Nursing.*

Kathleen O'Toole has combined a four-decade professional life in community organizing with writing. She received an M.A. from The Johns Hopkins University and has taught writing at Hopkins and at The Maryland Institute College of Art. Her poems have appeared widely in magazines and journals, including *America, The Christian Century, Notre Dame Review, Poetry, Poetry East, Potomac Review,* and *Prairie Schooner.* Her chapbook, *Practice,* was published in 2005 and was followed in 2011 by her first full-length collection, *Meanwhile.*

Made in the USA
Middletown, DE
05 March 2017